The Work People Do
AUTO MECHANIC

ACKNOWLEDGMENTS

Several people generously allowed me to photograph them at their work. I would like to thank Nasimul Bacchus, Michael Cheatham, Robert DeBlasio, Ward Filipon, Tony Laubis, Kennard Patterson, Lawrence Pfaff, Robert Schnibbe, and Kathleen Taylor.

Additionally, I want to thank Jessica Levy, Monroe Community College, Rochester, NY; Fred Allen and Doug Welsh, Brookdale Community College, Lincroft, NJ; George Anastos and Louis Orofino at Curry Acura, Scarsdale, NY; Marty Rheingold and Bernice Lefkowitz at West Holme Auto Service, Long Beach, NY; Bob's Service Station, Hastings-on-Hudson, NY; Lisa Ellrodt; Githa and Maria Ong; Lee Howe; my editor, Jane Steltenpohl; and my husband, Jim.

The Work People Do

ANIMAL DOCTOR
AUTO MECHANIC

JULIAN MESSNER and colophon are trademarks of Simon & Schuster, Inc.
Design by Sylvia Frezzolini and Michèle Goycoolea
Manufactured in the United States of America.

LIB. ED.   10 9 8 7 6 5 4 3 2 1
PAPER ED.   10 9 8 7 6 5 4 3 2 1

Library of Congress Cataloging-in-Publication Data
Imershein, Betsy.   The work people do: auto mechanic/by Betsy Imershein.
Summary: Introduces the occupation of being an auto mechanic and explains how many common tasks in that job are performed.   1. Automobile mechanics—Juvenile literature.   2. Automobiles—Maintenance and repair—Vocational guidance—Juvenile literature. [1. Automobile mechanics. 2. Automobiles—Maintenance and repair.   3. Occupations.]   I. Title.
TL152.I45   1989   89-12148
629.28'72'023   dc20   CIP
ISBN 0-671-68184-2   ISBN 0-671-68187-7 (pbk.)   AC

For my daughter, Zoe,
with love

The Work People Do
AUTO MECHANIC

by Betsy Imershein

JULIAN MESSNER

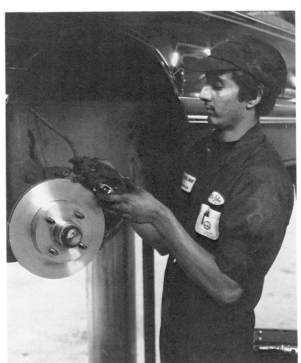

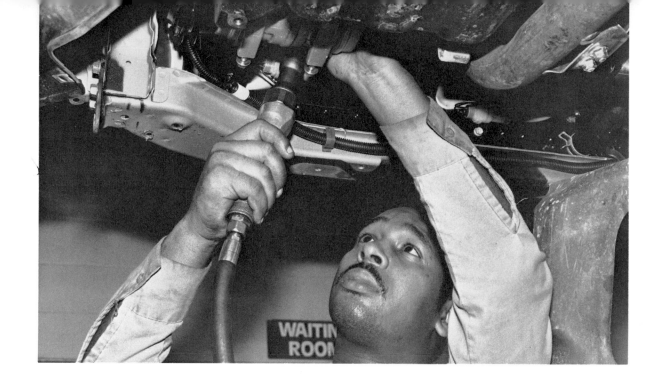

Kathy, Tony, John, Mike, and Kenny are auto mechanics, also called auto technicians. Auto mechanics love cars and love working on cars.

Cars take us almost everywhere we want to go. We couldn't do without them. They are machines with many parts that need regular care and attention.

Sometimes even with that care, cars break down or stop working as well as they should. So auto technicians, the people who keep our cars running, have very important jobs.

People become auto mechanics in different ways. Most mechanics take special courses in high school and college. Cars are one of their main courses of study.

Others love cars so much that they teach themselves everything possible about their family car. When they are old enough, they get a job working with cars.

Either way, there is a lot to know and to keep learning because cars change every year, and every car is different.

Auto mechanics work in different places. Kathy, Tony, and John work in a neighborhood garage. Garages usually have customers who live nearby. Mike and Kenny work at a dealership. Dealerships are where new cars are sold and where people often bring their cars back for servicing.

Some mechanics work at garages that also have gas stations. So if they are not busy working on cars, they might pump gas or tow a car that is in trouble.

Cars can't talk to us, so technicians have to use their knowledge and skill to diagnose, or figure out, what problem each car is having. Car owners can give them clues, which is a beginning. Once the mechanics have figured out the problem, they have to know how to fix it.

This car was brought in when the owner smelled gas and was afraid to keep driving. Kathy investigated.

She checked the fuel line, the fuel tank, and the smells of the car. Kathy decided that the fumes smelled like raw gas. That meant there was something wrong in the exhaust system.

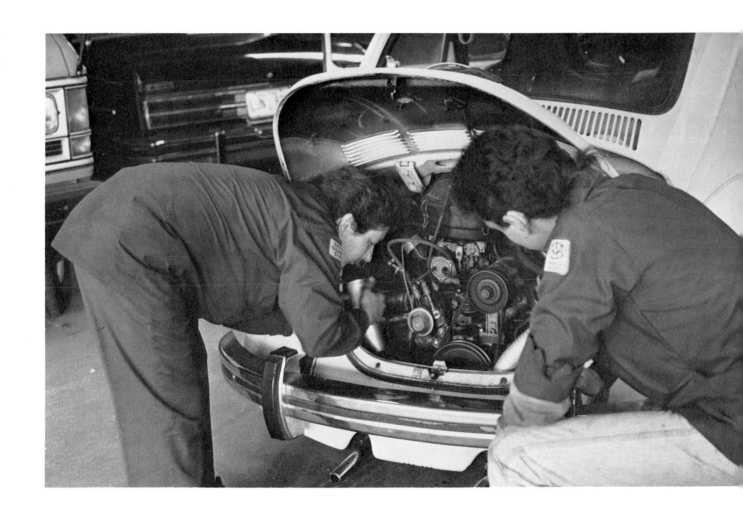

She hooked the car up to a special machine called an emissions analyzer to let it tell her exactly what the problem was. Then the machine printed out the information.

It's not possible for technicians to know exact details for every car. Kathy checked a special book to compare it to information from the machine. She found that one of the gas readings was off. From this she knew that the carburetor, which mixes air and gas, needed adjustment.

After Kathy adjusted the carburetor, she
rechecked the car to make sure the new readings
were correct. Then the customer was called to come
pick up the car.

Getting to all the parts of a car isn't easy. Technicians say that a car is never at the right height. They always wish it were a little higher or a little lower. Kenny raised the car on a lift to make his work easier.

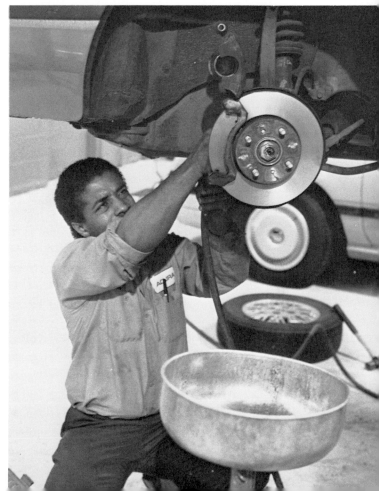

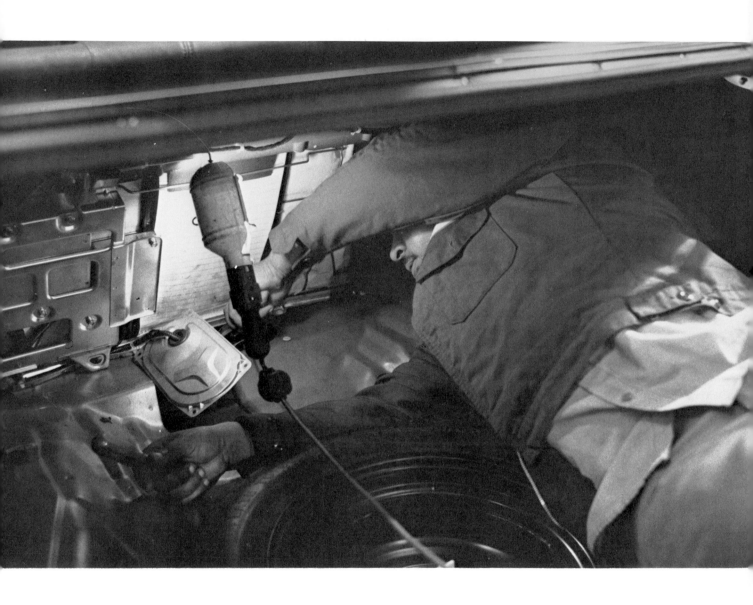

Sometimes the part they need to work on is not easy to reach. Mike had to climb into the trunk of this car to unscrew the gas tank, which needed replacement.

Since technicians end up in tight and awkward places, they must often work by touch alone. This is a difficult skill to learn and takes lots of practice.

Tools are another important part of an auto technician's work. Large machines, computers, and some specialized tools are owned by the garage or dealership. But technicians have to buy their own tools, which cost thousands of dollars. Then they must keep them in good working order.

And they need
a lot of tools.
Technicians are
constantly stopping
their work because
they need a
different one.
It seems as if
each screw and
part demands
its own tool.

Larry, the tool man, visits garages weekly to find out what new tools are needed and what tools need repair. Many can be fixed; some must be replaced.

Kathy and Tony usually check out new tools in Larry's van when he comes, though they don't always buy any.

As you can see, being a mechanic means getting very dirty and staying that way all day long. Mike is using a special soap, called Go-Jo soap, which takes off the grease and dirt.

Mechanics usually have a rag hanging out of a pocket, ready to wipe off the grease. But mechanics are people who enjoy working with their hands and don't mind getting dirty.

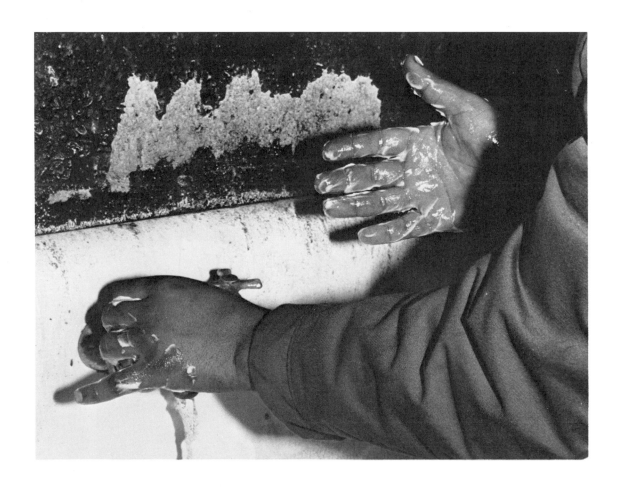

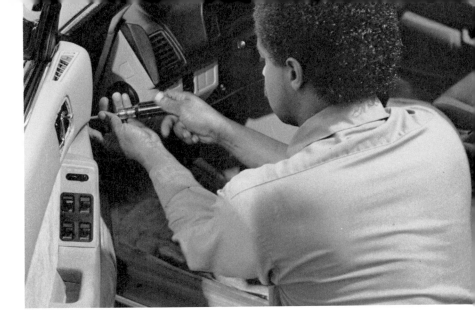

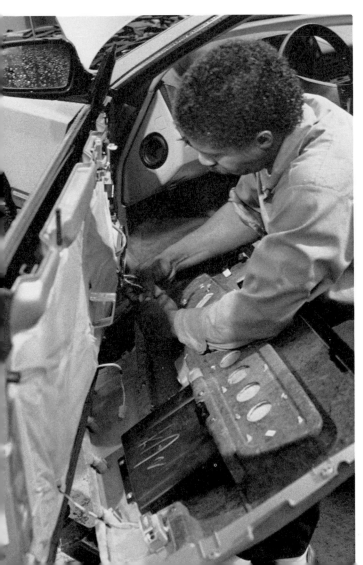

This car was brought in with the driver's door pocket broken. Kenny had to remove the inside door panel to replace it. Many screws needed to be loosened and then tightened when the panel was put back on. This was a slow but easy job for Kenny.

Not all jobs are easy. Cars are extremely heavy and some of their individual parts are very heavy, too. Auto technicians need to be strong and willing to lift and struggle with heavy equipment all day long, as Tony did here. This is a very tiring part of their work. But it's part of the challenge as well.

Customers are not allowed in the service area because it can be dangerous. The service area, or service department, is where cars are worked on by technicians.

Here, John is wearing a face mask for protection, and Kathy is wearing safety goggles. Injuries do happen, though not very often.

Many cars are not air-conditioned when people buy them. Mike put an air conditioner in this new car. Many pieces needed to be removed for the air conditioner to fit in the right places.

Mike did most of the work in the front of the car, but some needed to be done inside, too. He installed part of the unit under the glove compartment and a new button on the dashboard. The car was then put back together.

29

Auto mechanics never know what the day will bring. Each day brings new cars with new problems. Solving the problems and getting the cars working again make being a mechanic an important and satisfying job.

ABOUT THE AUTHOR

BETSY IMERSHEIN grew up in New York and holds a master's degree in social work from Yeshiva University. She studied photography at the International Center of Photography, Parsons School of Design, Cooper Union, and the Center for Nature Photography.

Ms. Imershein's other books include *When You Go To Kindergarten* (1986), *Animal Doctor* (1988), and *Finding Red/Finding Yellow* (1989). She lives with her husband, James Howe, and daughter, Zoe, in Hastings-on-Hudson, New York.